D0579615

Dalmatians are known for their spots

Dalmatians

Jean Allen

A+
Smart Apple Media

COPYRIGHT

🐾 Published by Smart Apple Media

1980 Lookout Drive, North Mankato, MN 56003

Designed by Rita Marshall

Copyright © 2004 Smart Apple Media. International copyright reserved in all countries. No part of this book may be reproduced in any form without written permission from the publisher.

Printed in the United States of America

🐾 Photographs by Barbara Augello, dogpix.com (Larry Reynolds), Getty Images (Tim Davis/Stone), Hulton Archive, The Image Finders (Patti McConville)

🐾 Library of Congress Cataloging-in-Publication Data

Allen, Jean. Dalmatians / by Jean Allen.

p. cm. – (Dog breeds) Summary: Introduces the physical characteristics, life cycle, breeding, training, and care of dalmatians. Includes instructions for a related activity.

🐾 ISBN 1-58340-317-5

1. Dalmatian dog–Juvenile literature. [1. Dalmatian dog. 2. Dogs.] I. Title. II. Series.

SF429.D3L64 2003   636.72–dc21   2002042808

🐾 First Edition 9 8 7 6 5 4 3 2 1

Dalmatians

CONTENTS

Firehouse Dogs

A team of horses races down the crowded street, pulling a fire engine. A white dog with black spots runs alongside them. Bells clang as people hurry to get out of the way. Smoke pours out of a building just down the block. Fire!

The horses reach the building, and the firefighters set up their equipment. Suddenly, the dog looks up and starts barking. A man on the third floor is leaning out of a window.

He is trapped! The firefighters rush to help the man escape.

Horse-drawn fire engines in the early 1900s

The dog—a Dalmatian—is the hero of the day. Dalmatians are best known as "firehouse dogs." They started helping firefighters in London, England, in the 1800s. At first, the dogs were used to catch rats in firehouses. Eventually they started racing alongside the horse-drawn fire engines. The dogs protected the horses from other dogs and

Dalmatians were used to guard American soldier camps during World War I, World War II, and the Vietnam War.

thieves while the firefighters worked. Today, Dalmatians are the mascots, or good-luck symbols, of many fire departments

Some firefighters keep Dalmatians as mascots

Dalmatians can run a long time without tiring

around the world. Dalmatians are very smart and can be trained to do many other jobs, too. In some countries, Dalmatians are sheepherders. Dalmatians are also popular hunting dogs, thanks to their sharp sense of smell and quickness in the field. They have lots of energy and can work and play all day.

Puppies to Dogs

Female Dalmatians usually give birth to **litters** of two to four pups. Surprisingly, Dalmatians are born without spots! The spots appear as the puppies grow up. When a Dalmatian is

fully grown, the spots range from one-half to one inch (1.3–2.5 cm) in size. 🐕 About 12 percent of Dalmatians are born completely deaf. Unfortunately, the deafness cannot be treated.

A Dalmatian puppy's spots get bigger as it grows

Deaf dogs are easily startled, and if surprised, they may bite.

Because of this, the Dalmatian Club of America believes that

deaf Dalmatian puppies should be **euthanized**.

Dalmatian puppies are **weaned** at **Dalmatians with brown spots are "liver-spotted." Some litters have both black-spotted and liver-spotted puppies.**

six to eight weeks of age. They are

fully grown at about a year. Adult

Dalmatians are tall dogs, standing 19

to 24 inches (48–60 cm) at the shoulder. They weigh from 40

to 70 pounds (18–32 kg). Males are usually larger than

females. With good care, a Dalmatian can live 11 to 13 years.

Dalmatian History

Some people think Dalmatians were first raised in ancient Egypt. Others believe the dogs came from a place

Male Dalmatians are usually taller than females

called Dalmatia (a region of Croatia on the Adriatic Sea) in the 1500s. Nobody knows for sure. Dalmatians have been around at least 400 years, because the dogs can be seen in paintings from the mid-1600s. Some

Dalmatians are very popular in England, where the dogs are sometimes called "plum pudding dogs."

paintings show Dalmatians working in England as coach dogs. These fast, strong animals were trained to run beside (or under) horse-drawn coaches, or carriages. When the carriage stopped, the Dalmatian guarded it while the master

Dalmatians are smart, loyal, watchful dogs

was away. Those skills eventually made the Dalmatian the perfect "firehouse dog." 🐕 Dalmatians are older than many other popular dog **breeds**. German shepherds, for example, were first raised a little more than 100 years ago.

Dalmatians as Pets

Dalmatians are friendly dogs, but they can be shy around strangers. They usually get along well with other dogs and pets. Dalmatians are very energetic and need exercise several times a day. It is important for owners to find an open field or yard in which they can play. 🐕 Dalmatian puppies

need a lot of training to learn to behave. They like to jump, and

because they are fairly large, they can easily knock down a

child during play. Dalmatians **shed** a lot and should be

Dalmatian puppies love to play

brushed every day. They should also be bathed every three to four months. High-quality dog food has a lot of meat in it and can help keep a Dalmatian healthy. The dog should also have fresh water available at all times. Dalmatians are best known as "firehouse dogs," but they can be loyal, loving pets. If given a lot of love, attention, and exercise, Dalmatians can be excellent companions for children and adults.

A man reportedly counted all the spots on the dogs in the 1961 movie *101 Dalmatians*. He counted 6,469,952!

A healthy, full-grown Dalmatian

Spotted Treats

You and your friends can make a whole litter of spotted snacks that are as much fun to look at as they are to eat!

What You Need

Flour tortillas

A squeeze bottle of chocolate syrup

Raisins

Chocolate chips

Red-colored jam or jelly

A dull butter knife

What You Do

1. Using the knife, carefully cut a dog shape out of each tortilla.

2. Using chocolate syrup as glue, place the chocolate chips as the dogs' eyes and the raisins as the noses. Dab a little jam to make mouths or tongues.

3. Hold the bottle of chocolate syrup a few inches above the tortilla dogs. Gently squeeze it, making spots all over the dogs.

4. Eat your Dalmatian treats!

Each Dalmatian has a unique set of spots

I N F O R M A T I O N

Index

Words to Know

breeds (BREEDZ)—types of dogs, such as poodles, collies, or bulldogs

coach (KOHCH)—a vehicle pulled by horses; also called a carriage

euthanized (YOO-thun-eyezd)—painlessly put to death so that the animal does not suffer

litters (LITT-urz)—groups of puppies born at the same time

shed (SHED)—to lose hair a little at a time

weaned (WEEND)—when a puppy stops drinking its mother's milk and starts eating other foods

Read More

Kallen, Stuart A. *Dalmatians.* New York: Checkerboard Library, 1996.

Mars, Julie. *Dalmatians.* Kansas City, Mo.: Andrews and McMeel, 1996.

Murray, Julie. *Dalmatians.* Edina, Minn.: Abdo & Daughters, 2002.

Internet Sites

American Kennel Club: Dalmatian
http://www.akc.org/breeds/recbreeds/
dalmati.cfm

Sparky the Fire Dog
http://www.nfpa.org/sparky

Dalmatian Club of America
http://www.thedca.org